This book is dedicated to
all of those who never got
to fully embrace their culture,
and to the ones who just need
a little inspiration to do so.

Love,

Matisse

Matisse Azul
and the
Magic Shoes

Words by:

Matisse Azul Rainbolt

&

Ryan Wade Rainbolt Sr.

Pictures by:

Riley S. Quinn

Edited By:

William J. Tynan

When Matisse Azul was four years old, she really wanted to dance. She told her parents, and they enrolled her in ballet lessons.

Matisse enjoyed twisting her body into different shapes, but the sound of the classical music and the slow bobbing movements made her eyes feel heavy and her mouth want to yawn.

Ballet **wasn't** the right kind of dancing for Matisse.

Matisse tried tap dancing next. She liked the way her feet stayed busy with the sounds of clicks and snaps, bumps and thwaps.

Tap dancing made it sound like her feet were playing the drums, but her right arm felt left out, and her left arm couldn't find its right place.

Tap **wasn't** the right kind of dancing for Matisse, either.

Then one day, while enjoying *elote* at the county fair, Matisse saw the most beautiful dancers she had ever seen. In fact, she could not take her eyes off of them. Matisse was hypnotized by the swirling patterns of color, ribbon, and lace she saw in their *vestidos*.

As they danced, Matisse bounced to the rhythm of their stomping feet and immediately knew that this **was** the right kind of dancing for her!

The dancing combined the beauty and grace of ballet with the rhythm and energy of tap. Matisse felt a connection with the dancers that she didn't quite understand.

"Matisse, do you like this dancing?" her mommy asked.
"Oh, yes," she said. "I love it! It's beautiful!"

"This is a traditional dance from Mexico," her mommy told her, "the country of your ancestors. It's called *ballet folklórico*."

After seeing how excited Matisse was about her experience at the fair, her parents took her to visit a ballet folklórico dance group.

When they arrived, Matisse hid behind her mommy's leg, watching and wondering what it would be like to dance the way they did.

"I want to learn, mommy," whispered Matisse. "I want to be a ballet folklórico dancer." Her mommy smiled.

Matisse was ready to try. Her mommy helped her put on a pair of borrowed *zapatos* and a hand-made skirt. She began to practice with the other dancers her age, but quickly felt nervous and unsure. Feeling self-conscious, Matisse whispered to her mommy, "They already know how to dance." Tears filled her eyes. Matisse said, "I want to go home."

A few days later, Matisse decided to give ballet folklórico another try. However, when she arrived for her second practice she quickly began to feel uneasy. Her tummy was turning in circles, like the colorful folklórico skirts she loved so much.

"I think I'll just watch this time," she said, once again peeking out from behind her mommy.

Suddenly, a few of the dancers came over to her. "Come on, Matisse," they encouraged her, "¡*Vamos a bailar!*" Looking up at her smiling mommy, her twirling tummy calmed down. Matisse decided to join the other dancers. She studied their steps, mimicked their movements, and tried her best to copy everything they did. Just as Matisse was starting to feel confident, she slipped and fell in front of everyone.

She felt so embarrassed, but this time Matisse did not quit. She got right back up and rejoined the other dancers who helped her learn the dance, step-by-step.

Feeling encouraged by her teacher and all of the other dancers, Matisse started practicing at home. She practiced before breakfast, all afternoon, and every evening until she learned the dance by heart.

Her teacher was very pleased. "You have done so well, Matisse. It is time for you to perform in a real show."

The day of the performance arrived, and Matisse was thrilled! She felt as though butterflies were fluttering in her tummy. She was finally going to wear a real vestido, on a real stage, and perform for a real audience. Matisse was eager to create rippling waves of color with her beautiful skirt and stomp her feet to the rhythmic music.

Backstage, Matisse and the other dancers perfected their hair and make-up. Matisse looked into the mirror, took a deep breath, and smiled back at herself.

"It's time!" her teacher shouted. The dancers took their places offstage. The music began to play, filling the air with the traditional sounds of *Jalisco*.

At just the right moment, the dancers appeared onstage.
Matisse carefully tapped her toes and found her spot.

When she looked up, she saw a sea of people
waiting for a spectacular show to begin.

She felt everyone's eyes on her.
Suddenly, her legs wouldn't move, and her arms couldn't lift.
And once again, her eyes filled with tears and her tummy ached.

"I can't do it!" she cried,

and

ran

off

the

stage.

That night, Matisse climbed into bed feeling sad and worried that she had disappointed her teacher and fellow dancers. She whimpered and closed her eyes, wondering if she'd ever have the courage to dance again. At that moment, a beam of light streamed through her doorway. Matisse opened her eyes and looked up. There, standing in the light, was her mommy holding a small box behind her back.

A single tear rolled down Matisse's cheek. "I really wanted to be the best folklórico dancer," she said.

"I know, *mija*," her mommy said as she placed the small box on the bed. "I think I found something that will help." Matisse's mommy opened the box and revealed a pair of shiny, white folklórico shoes.

"I traveled a long way to find these," she said. "They are very special and rare. These are magic dancing shoes made especially for you. And look, they even have your name on them." Matisse stared at the brand-new shoes that seemed to sparkle and glow before her eyes.

She felt a rush of excitement, sprung out of bed, and quickly tied on her skirt. Her mommy helped buckle her new magic shoes. They fit perfectly! When she began to dance, her shoes made her *zapateado* sound perfect, and her *faldeo* came with an ease she had never experienced before.

Her smile grew bigger and bigger as she hugged her mommy tighter and tighter. "Thank you, thank you, thank you," she whispered into her mommy's ear.

That night, Matisse slept soundly. She dreamed of her mommy's journey to find the magic shoes. In her dream, she followed her mommy to a small shop on *Olvera Street*.

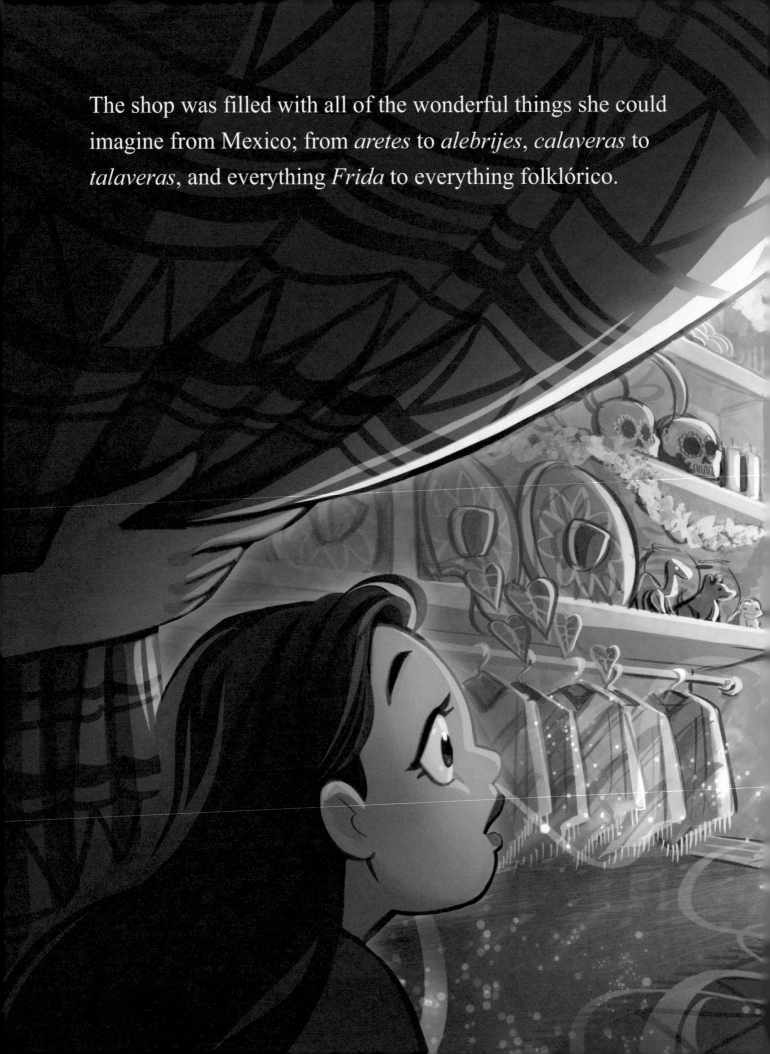

The shop was filled with all of the wonderful things she could imagine from Mexico; from *aretes* to *alebrijes*, *calaveras* to *talaveras*, and everything *Frida* to everything folklórico.

As her mommy pulled aside a large woven blanket that separated one room from another, they heard the song of a soft spoken man and the sad strumming of a *guitarra*. *"Bienvenidos. Pásale,"* he sang out to them.

A beam of light shined on the man standing behind the counter. When the light hit his face, Matisse could see that he looked just like her great-grandpa, Manuel!

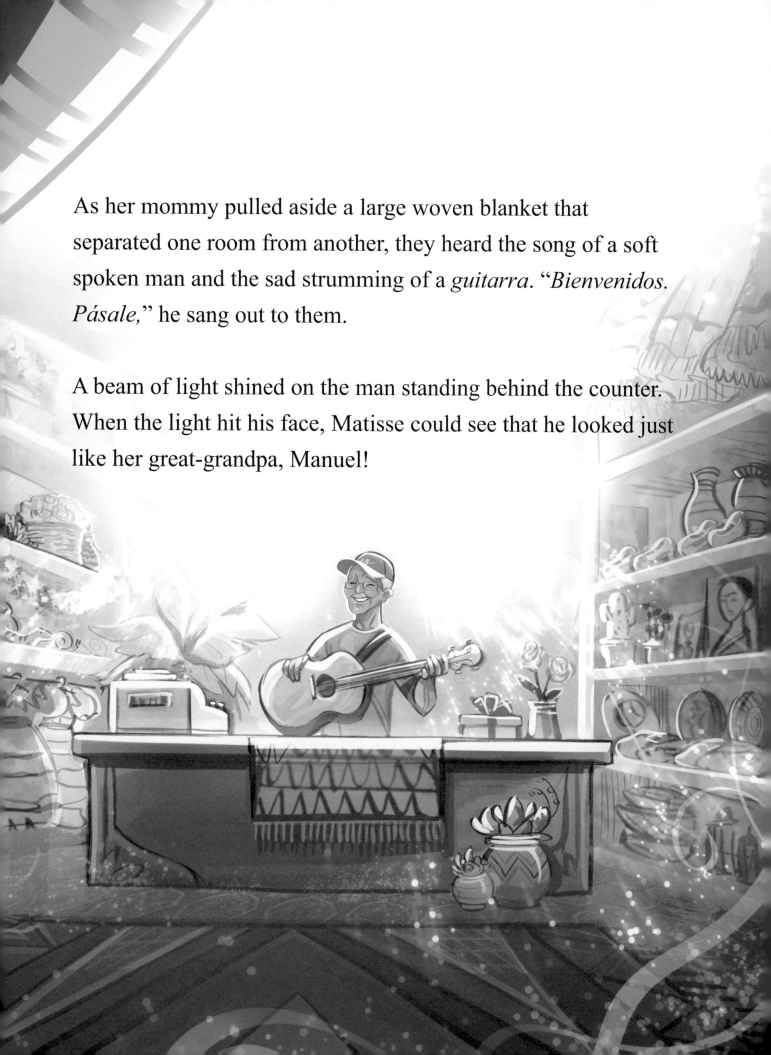

"It's a message from my ancestors," Matisse whispered to herself
as she snapped awake from a deep sleep.
"They want me to dance ballet folklórico in my magic shoes!"

Matisse could not wait to get back to folklórico practice and use her magic shoes. When she arrived, she put them on quickly and danced all around.

"*Mírate*, Matisse!" laughed her instructor. "I'm impressed. I can tell you have been practicing. Look how far you've come. I think it's time to begin rehearsing a solo performance for next month's show."

"Oh, thank you!" said Matisse, beaming with pride. "I can't wait!"

At the next show, Matisse danced skillfully and with grace. Her solo performance was incredible, and the crowd loved it. There were many *gritos* and a standing ovation. Matisse sparkled with happiness and took her bow.

There, in the front row, she saw her great-grandma Lucy smiling proudly with tears in her eyes. Matisse could feel her great-grandpa Manuel there in the audience, too.

Matisse looked down and whispered, "Thank you, magic shoes," as the smiles from the crowd washed over her.

As Matisse danced more and more, her confidence grew and grew, and so did her feet! One day, after another wonderful performance, Matisse struggled to take off her shoes. Her feet ached and the bottom of each toe felt like it had been stung by a bee.

"My feet hurt," said Matisse. Her mommy pushed against the tip of Matisse's shoes and then gently pulled them off. Gasping, she said, "Oh, no, Matisse! These blisters tell me that you've outgrown your shoes."

That night, Matisse carefully crawled into bed with a bandage wrapped around almost every toe. She pulled the covers to her chin and closed her eyes. As she began to drift off to sleep, she heard the door open.

Her mommy came in, sat down on the edge of her bed, and placed another box in front of her. Matisse excitedly removed the lid to discover a brand-new pair of shoes in her new, bigger size. "You got me another pair of magic shoes?!"

Her mommy smiled softly and said, "No, Matisse. These shoes are not magic."

Suddenly, the all too familiar ache returned to Matisse's tummy and tears came to her eyes.

"Dancing will never be the same again," Matisse sobbed.

Her mommy listened patiently and finally said, "Matisse, the time has come for me to tell you the truth. Your old shoes were not magic, either."

"What do you mean?" asked Matisse. "I could only dance so well because of the magic shoes!"

"No, mija. The story of the magic shoes was a way to help you start believing in yourself. The real magic has always lived inside of you. It is a gift your ancestors brought with them from Mexico many years ago. All you needed was the courage to let it out.

Matisse placed her old "magic shoes" on a shelf
as a reminder to believe in herself.

From that day forward she used the magic
that she now knew came from within,
to dance and make people smile.

Over the years, Matisse performed for audiences around the world,
showcasing the cultural beauty and timeless traditions of Mexico.
After each bow, she thanked her ancestors for all they had given her.

Matisse grew up to become a dance teacher. Now, when she sees a child doubting the magic inside of them, she shares the story of *Matisse Azul and the Magic Shoes.*

The End

Glossary

Alebrijes (ah-leh-bree-hehs) are brightly colored Mexican folk art sculptures depicting fantastical animals or creatures. They are often believed to be spirits that guide, protect, and accompany people throughout their lives.

Aretes (ah-reh-tehs) is the Spanish word for earrings. You'll notice Matisse is wearing hoop earrings in many of the illustrations throughout this book.

Ballet Folklórico (bah-ley fohl-kloh-ree-koh) is a dance form that combines music, dancing, and traditional attire to depict the history, cultures, beliefs, stories, and rich cultural heritage of different indigenous groups from across Mexico. The art form is passed down from generation to generation and performed at cultural festivals, celebrations, and events both in Mexico and around the world.

Bienvenidos (be-yen-beh-nee-dohs) is the Spanish word for welcome. It is a respectful word to use when inviting someone into your home, school, business, game, or activity.

Calaveras (kah-lah-beh-rahs) is the Spanish word for skulls. Skulls made out of sugar are used during Día De Los Muertos, or Day of the Dead, to help celebrate the lives of family and friends who have passed away.

Elote (eh-loh-teh) means "corn cob" in Spanish. Mexican elote is grilled corn on the cob that is oftentimes slathered in a mayonnaise and flavored with chili powder, cheese, and lime. Elotes are commonly sold from street carts for a tasty meal to go.

Faldeo (fall-day-oh) is the Spanish word for the movements of the ballet folklórico skirt created by the choreographed movements of the arms and hands.

Frida (free-dah) is a reference to Frida Kahlo, a very well-known Mexican artist known for her many striking paintings, including portraits, murals, and other works of art inspired by the nature and artifacts of Mexico. She became an icon through her character, activism, and unique style of art.

Gritos (gree-tohs) is the Spanish word for shouts. In Mexican culture, gritos are often used to express emotion or appreciation for events that are occurring.

Guitarra (gee-tah-rrah) is the Spanish word for guitar. It's an example of a cognate. Cognates are words that sound the same, or similar, in both English and Spanish.

Jalisco (hah-lees-koh) is the name of one of the thirty-two states of Mexico. It is known all over the world for its many cultural contributions in art, music, dance, and more.

Mija (mee-hah) is Spanish for "my daughter," but is also used to communicate words such as "dear," "honey," or "sweetheart."

Mírate (mee-dah-teh) is the Spanish word for the English phrase, "Look at you."

Olvera (olh-veh-ruh) **Street** is located in downtown Los Angeles, CA., and was founded in 1781. Known to many as, "the birthplace of Los Angeles," it's where the city's first church, firehouse, and theatre are located. It is a narrow, tree-shaded, brick-lined, pedestrian only Mexican marketplace with old structures, painted stalls, street vendors, cafes, restaurants, and gift shops selling handcrafted goods and Mexican folk art.

Pásale (pah-sah-leh) is a Spanish word that means, "Come in." It is a more informal way of inviting someone to enter a place or space.

Talaveras (tah-lah-beh-rahs) are handcrafted works of art, mainly created in the state of Puebla, Mexico. The techniques used to create these objects have been passed down from generation to generation for hundreds of years. You'll recognize them by their colorfully painted shapes and floral patterns.

Vamos a bailar (bah-mohs ah by-lahr) is a Spanish phrase that means, "Let's dance." It is often used during parties and other celebrations.

Vestido (behs-tee-doh) is the Spanish word for dress. Traditionally, the female ballet folklórico dancers wear dresses unique to each region of Mexico.

Zapateado (sah-pah-teh-ah-doh) is the Spanish word for the rhythmic tapping and stomping of the shoes. Notice the word zapato is in the word zapateado.

Zapatos (sah-pah-tohs) is the Spanish word for shoes. There are many styles of folklórico shoes, but one thing that most have in common are tiny nails hammered into the bottom that help make different sounds as the dances are performed.

Matisse Azul Rainbolt (age 4)
and her mommy

Matisse Azul Rainbolt
(age 23)

'Matisse Azul and the Magic Shoes' is inspired by the life of Matisse Azul Rainbolt, a professional ballet folklórico dancer and dance instructor from San Bernardino, California. Born in 2001, Matisse began her folklórico journey at four years old. By eleven, she was already sharing her passion for traditional Mexican dancing by teaching ballet folklórico to other students in her elementary school's after-school program. At fifteen, she began teaching in the community-based folklórico group that is mentioned in this book.

Driven by her love for dance and desire to bring joy to others, Matisse founded Step-By-Step Folklórico in 2023, a company dedicated to providing ballet folklórico lessons and cultural arts education to children of all ages. Through her leadership, Matisse and her team have impacted the lives of thousands of children by promoting cultural pride, personal expression, and the joy of dancing.